The Shadow of a Boy

Gary Owen's first play, *Crazy Gary's Mobile Disco*, was directed by Vicky Featherstone for Paines Plough and Sgript Cymru, and toured the UK in Spring 2001. His third, *The Drowned World*, is joint winner of the George Devine award and opens in August 2002 at the Traverse Theatre (Paines Plough). His first Welsh play, *Amser Canser*, will be produced by the Welsh College of Music and Drama early in 2003. Gary's first radio play, *The Island of the Blessed*, is to be broadcast in July 2002 as part of *The Wire* on Radio 3.

by the same author

Crazy Gary's Mobile Disco

The Shadow of a Boy

Gary Owen

Methuen Drama

Published by Methuen 2002

1 3 5 7 9 10 8 6 4 2

First published in 2002 by
Methuen Publishing Limited,
215 Vauxhall Bridge Road,
London SW1V 1EJ

Methuen Publishing Limited Reg. No. 3543167

A CIP catalogue record is available from the British Library

ISBN 0 413 77208 X

Typeset by SX Composing DTP, Rayleigh, Essex
Printed and bound in Great Britain by
Cox & Wyman Ltd, Reading, Berkshire

The Shadow of a Boy

by Gary Owen

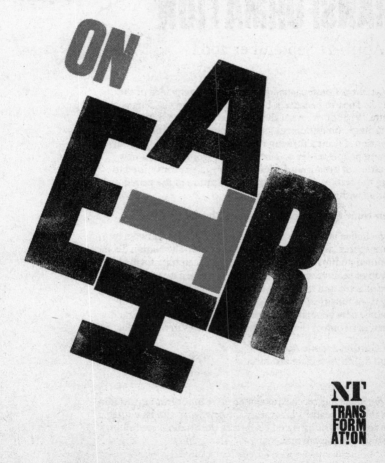

NT
TRANS
FORM
AT!ON

TRANSFORMATION

29 April–21 September 2002

The Lyttelton *Transformation* project is vital to my idea of the National Theatre because it both celebrates and challenges our identity. What do we want the National to be? We must draw on our heritage, on our recent past, and on the talent of the next generation. I want a thriving new audience, including a body of young people under 30 with a theatre-going habit, a new generation of artistic and administrative talent committed to taking the National forward and a realization of the varied potential within this glorious building.

Trevor Nunn Director of the National Theatre

Transformation is thirteen world premieres, hosted in two new theatre spaces, with special low ticket prices. The National's most traditional auditorium, the Lyttelton, has been transformed by a sweep of seats from circle to stage to create a new intimacy between actor and audience. At the same time the Loft has been created – a fully flexible 100-seat theatre. *Transformation* will introduce new generations of theatre makers and theatre audiences to one of the most exciting theatres in the world.

Mick Gordon Artistic Associate
Joseph Smith Associate Producer

Transformation has received major creative input from the Studio – the National Theatre's laboratory for new work and its engine room for new writing – and celebrates the Studio's continuing investment in theatre makers.

The Shadow of a Boy

by Gary Owen

In order of speaking

Luke	ROB STORR
Katie	CATRIN RHYS
Nanna	LYNN HUNTER
Shadow	JO STONE-FEWINGS
Director	ERICA WHYMAN
Designer	SOUTRA GILMOUR
Lighting Designer	STEVE BARNETT
Sound Designer	RICH WALSH
Company Voice Work	PATSY RODENBURG & KATE GODFREY
Production Manager	Katrina Gilroy
Stage Manager	Emma B Lloyd
Deputy Stage Manager	Thomas Vowles
Assistant Stage Manager	Mary O'Hanlon
Costume Supervisor	Frances Gager, assisted by Louise Bratton
Casting	Maggie Lunn

OPENING: Loft, 17 June 2002

The *Shadow of a Boy* is supported by
the Peter Wolff Theatre Trust

Peter Wolff
THEATRE TRUST

Copies of this cast list in braille or large print are available at the Information Desk

LYNN HUNTER
NANNA

Theatre includes Kiss on the Bottom (Grace), A Letter from Sarajevo (Mercury), Family Planning (Grass Roots), Under Milk Wood (Sherman/UK & USA), Cluedo (Torch), Branwen (Made in Wales), Hiawatha (Torch). **TV** includes Into the Void, Tales from the Pleasure Beach, Care, Casualty, Civvies, Morphine and Dolly Mixtures. **Film** includes Arthur's Dyke, Very Annie-Mary, House, Restoration. **Radio** includes Station Road, A Child's Christmas in Wales, The Mask of Zorro, Skeletons.

CATRIN RHYS
KATIE

Trained at Welsh College of Music and Drama. **Theatre** includes To Kill A Mocking Bird, Flora's War, Accidental Death of an Anarchist, Hard Times, Alexander Cordell Trilogy, Under Milk Wood (Theatr Clwyd), Sleepers' Den (Southwark), A Prayer for Wings (Torch Theatre). **TV** includes Score, Pacio. **Radio** includes Miranda in The Tempest, Waves in the Chat Room, Station Road.

JO STONE-FEWINGS
SHADOW

Theatre includes Ghetto, War and Peace, Fuente Ovejuna (NT); King John, Twelfth Night, Henry VI, The Battle for the Throne, The Park, Henry VIII, The Merry Wives of Windsor, Cymbeline, Richard III, The Taming of the Shrew (RSC); The Importance of Being Earnest (Manchester Royal Exchange); One Over The Eight (Stephen Joseph Theatre Scarborough); The Misanthrope (Young Vic). **TV** includes Medics, Waiting for God, Shrinks, Moon & Son, The Prince, Peak Practice. **Film** includes American Friends, Deadly Advice, All the King's Men.

ROB STORR
LUKE

Trained at Welsh College of Music and Drama. **Theatre** includes Country of the Blind (Gate), Live Like Pigs (Bute, Cardiff), Silence (Stephen Joseph Theatre – Judges Commendation for Acting), The World Has Turned Upside Down (Sherman Theatre Cardiff), Hated Nightfall, AC/DC (Bethseilun, Aberystwyth), Titus in Titus Andronicus (Castle Theatre, Aberystwyth) and Caucasian Chalk Circle (National Youth Theatre of Wales)

ERICA WHYMAN
DIRECTOR

Artistic Director of The Gate Theatre, London. She was awarded the Cohen Bursary from the NT Studio in 1998. **Directing** credits include The Gambler, Oblomov (Pleasance, Edinburgh and London), To The Lighthouse (Bloomsbury), Blue Remembered Hills (Bristol Old Vic), The Glass Slipper, The Winter's Tale, The Old Curiosity Shop (Southwark), Tear from a Glass Eye, Les Justes, Box of Bananas and Ion (Gate), Fool for Love (ETT), Three Wishes by Ben Moor (Pleasance, Edinburgh) and The Birthday Party (Sheffield Crucible).

SOUTRA GILMOUR
DESIGNER

Theatre includes The Birthday Party (Crucible), Hand in Hand (Hampstead), Fool for Love (English Touring Theatre), Peter Pan (Tramway), Sun is Shining (King's Head), Tear from a Glass Eye, Les Justes (The Gate), The Woman Who Swallowed a Pin (Southwark Playhouse). **Opera** includes: A Better Place (ENO), La Boheme (Opera Ireland Touring), Eight Songs for a Mad King (National World Tour), El Cimarron (QEH, Southbank). Current work includes: Ion (Gate).

STEVE BARNETT
Lighting Designer

Lighting credits include *Sing Yer Heart Out for the Lads*, *Sparkleshark* (National), *Carmen* and *L'Elisir d'Amore* (Surrey Opera), *Bedroom Farce* and *Blithe Spirit* (Redgrave Theatre), *Sympathetic Magic* (Finborough), *La Venexiana* (Etcetera) and Evelyn Glennie's multi-media show *Shadow* touring UK and Europe. He has worked at many regional theatres and at the National since 1994. He relit *Frogs* (NT Education tour) and has been Assistant to the Lighting Designer on *My Fair Lady*, *The Winter's Tale*, *The Waiting Room*, *Mother Courage* and *Peter Pan*, relighting the revival.

RICH WALSH
Sound Designer

Previous sound designs include *Sing Yer Heart Out For the Lads*, *Free* and *The Walls* for the National; *Exposure*, *Under The Blue Sky*, *On Raftery's Hill*, *Sacred Heart*, *Trust*, *Choice* (Royal Court); *50 Revolutions* (Whitehall); *The Boy Who Left Home*, *The Nation's Favourite* (UK tours); *Yllana's 666* (Riverside Studios); *Strike Gently Away From Body*, *Blavatsky* (Young Vic Studio); *Body & Soul*, *Soap Opera*, *The Baltimore Waltz* (Upstairs at the Gatehouse); *Small Craft Warnings* (Pleasance); *The Taming of the Shrew* and *Macbeth* (Japanese tour).

PETER WOLFF THEATRE TRUST

The Peter Wolff Theatre Trust is delighted to be supporting *The Shadow of a Boy* by Gary Owen as part of the new writing venture in The Loft. The Trust was founded by Peter Wolff, a textile entrepreneur, who has had a great love of the British theatre all his life. In January 1998 he created the non-profit-making Trust to encourage the work of emerging British playwrights and to bring these plays to a wider audience. Since its foundation the Trust has supported fourteen new plays including *To The Green Fields Beyond* by Nick Whitby, *Splendour* by Abi Morgan and *Humble Boy* by Charlotte Jones. The Director of the Trust is Neal Foster.

The Loft Theatre was created with the help of the Royal National Theatre Foundation.

Many of the projects in the *Transformation* season were developed in the National Theatre Studio.

The Transformation season is supported by Edward and Elissa Annunziato, Peter Wolff Theatre Trust, and by a gift from the estate of André Deutsch.

ON WORD graphics designed by typographer Alan Kitching using original wood letters.

NATIONAL THEATRE BOOKSHOP

The National's Bookshop in the Main Entrance foyer on the ground floor stocks a wide range of theatre-related books. Texts of all plays in the Loft during the Transformation season, and of the plays in *Channels (France)* are available from the NT Bookshop at £2. Gary Owen's *Crazy Gary's Mobile Disco!* is also on sale.
T: 020 7452 3456; www.nationaltheatre.org.uk/bookshop

TRANSFORMATION SEASON TEAM (Loft)

ARTISTIC ASSOCIATE Mick Gordon
ASSOCIATE PRODUCER Joseph Smith
ADMINISTRATOR Sarah Nicholson
LOFT THEATRE DESIGNER Will Bowen
FRONT OF HOUSE DESIGNER Jo Maund
FRONT OF HOUSE DESIGN PRODUCTION MANAGER Gavin Gibson
LITERARY MANAGER Jack Bradley
PLANNING PROJECT MANAGER Paul Jozefowski
RESIDENT DIRECTOR – LOFT Paul Miller
PRODUCTION CO-ORDINATOR Katrina Gilroy
PRODUCTION MANAGER – LOFT REALISATION Jo Maund
PRODUCTION ASSISTANTS – LOFT REALISATION Alan Bain and Gavin Gibson
LOFT LIGHTING REALISATION & TECHNICIANS Mike Atkinson, Steve Barnett,
    Pete Bull, Huw Llewellyn, Cat Silver
LOFT SOUND REALISATION Adam Rudd, Rich Walsh
LOFT STAGE TECHNICIANS Danny O'Neill, Stuart Smith
MODEL MAKERS Aaron Marsden, Riette Hayes-Davies
GRAPHIC DESIGNERS Patrick Eley, Stephen Cummiskey
PROGRAMME EDITOR Dinah Wood
PRESS Lucinda Morrison, Mary Parker, Gemma Gibb
MARKETING David Hamilton-Peters
PRODUCTION PHOTOGRAPHER Sheila Burnett
THEATRE MANAGER John Langley

Thanks to the following people who were part of the original Lyttelton Development Group:
Ushi Bagga, Alice Dunne, Annie Eves-Boland, Jonathan Holloway, Gareth James,
Mark Jonathan, Holly Kendrick, Paul Jozefowski, Angus MacKechnie, Tim Redfern,
Chris Shutt, Matt Strevens, Jane Suffling, Nicola Wilson, Dinah Wood, Lucy Woollatt

The National's workshops are responsible for, on these productions:
Armoury; Costume; Props & furniture; Scenic construction; Scenic Painting; Wigs

TRANSFORMATION SEASON

IN THE LYTTELTON

A co-production between the National Theatre & Théâtre National de Chaillot

The PowerBook .... 9 May–4 June
from a novel by Jeanette Winterson
devised by Jeanette Winterson, Deborah Warner & Fiona Shaw
Director Deborah Warner

A Prayer for Owen Meany .... 10–29 June
a novel by John Irving
adapted by Simon Bent
Director Mick Gordon

A collaboration between the National Theatre & Trestle Theatre Company

The Adventures of the Stoneheads .... 4–13 July
written & directed by Toby Wilsher

A collaboration between the National Theatre & Mamaloucos Circus

The Birds .... 22 July–3 August
by Aristophanes, in a new version by Sean O'Brien
Director Kathryn Hunter

Play Without Words .... 20 August–14 September
devised & directed by Matthew Bourne

IN THE LOFT

Sing Yer Heart Out for the Lads .... 29 April–15 May
by Roy Williams
Director Simon Usher

Free .... 20 May–8 June
by Simon Bowen
Director Thea Sharrock

Life After Life .... 28 May–8 June
a reportage play by Paul Jepson & Tony Parker
Director Paul Jepson

The Shadow of a Boy .... 13–29 June
by Gary Owen
Director Erica Whyman

The Mentalists .... 4–20 July
by Richard Bean
Director Sean Holmes

Sanctuary .... 25 July–10 August
by Tanika Gupta
Director Hettie Macdonald

The Associate .... 15–31 August
by Simon Bent
Director Paul Miller

Closing Time .... 4–21 September
by Owen McCafferty
Director James Kerr

NATIONAL THEATRE STUDIO &
TRANSFORMATION

All the plays in the LOFT are co-produced with the National Theatre Studio. The Studio is the National's laboratory for research and development, providing a workspace outside the confines of the rehearsal room and stage, where artists can experiment and develop their skills.

As part of its training for artists there is an on-going programme of classes, workshops, seminars, courses and masterclasses. Residencies have also been held in Edinburgh, Vilnius, Belfast and South Africa, enabling artists from a wider community to share and exchange experiences.

Central to the Studio's work is a commitment to new writing. The development and support of writers is demonstrated through play readings, workshops, short-term attachments, bursaries and sessions with senior writers. Work developed there continually reaches audiences throughout the country and overseas, on radio, film and television as well as at the National and other theatres. Most recent work includes the award-winning plays *Further than the Furthest Thing* by Zinnie Harris (Tron Theatre, Glasgow; Traverse, Edinburgh, and NT), *The Waiting Room* by Tanika Gupta (NT) and *Gagarin Way* by Gregory Burke (in association with Traverse, Edinburgh; NT; and at the Arts Theatre), *The Walls* by Colin Teevan (NT), *Accomplices* by Simon Bent, *Mr England* by Richard Bean (in association with Sheffield Theatres) and *The Slight Witch* by Paul Lucas (in association with Birmingham Rep), as well as a season of five new plays from around the world with the Gate Theatre, and *Missing Reel* by Toby Jones at the Traverse during the Edinburgh Festival 2001. *Gagarin Way* and *Further than the Furthest Thing* were part of SPRINGBOARDS – a series of partnerships created by the Royal National Theatre Studio with other theatres, enabling work by emerging writers to reach a wider audience.

Direct Action, a collaboration between The Studio and the Young Vic, is an initiative that provides young directors with an opportunity to work on the main stage of the Young Vic. Two plays were co-produced in the autumn of 2001: Max Frisch's *Andorra*, directed by Gregory Thompson; and David Rudkin's *Afore Night Come*, directed by Rufus Norris, who won the Evening Standard award for Best Newcomer for this production.

For the Royal National Theatre Studio

HEAD OF STUDIO	Sue Higginson
STUDIO MANAGER	Matt Strevens
TECHNICAL MANAGER	Eddie Keogh
INTERNATIONAL PROJECTS MANAGER	Philippe Le Moine

Royal National Theatre
South Bank, London SE1 9PX
Box Office: 020 7452 3000
Information: 020 7452 3400

Registered Charity No: 224223

The chief aims of the National, under the direction of Trevor Nunn, are to present a diverse repertoire, embracing classic, new and neglected plays; to present these plays to the very highest standards; and to give audiences a wide choice.

All kinds of other events and services are on offer – short early-evening Platform performances; work for children and education work; free live entertainment both inside and outdoors at holiday times; exhibitions; live foyer music; backstage tours; bookshops; plenty of places to eat and drink; and easy car-parking. The nearby Studio acts as a resource for research and development for actors, writers and directors.

We send productions on tour, both in this country and abroad, and do all we can, through ticket-pricing, to make the NT accessible to everyone.

The National's home on the South Bank, opened in 1976, contains three separate theatres: the Olivier, the Lyttelton, and the Cottesloe and – during Transformation – a fourth: the Loft. It is open to the public all day, six days a week, fifty-two weeks a year. Stage by Stage – an exhibition on the NT's history, can be seen in the Olivier Gallery.

This play is for
Jan Morgan
David Owen
Peter Morgan
and for my nanna, Teresa Hughes

Acknowledgements

My thanks to Alison Hindell, David Britton, Sally Baker and all at Ty Newydd; to Jack Bradley, Sue Higginson, David Eldridge, Paul Miller and the National Theatre Studio; to Michael McCoy; to Andrea Smith and Andy Sperling for giving me a place to stay. And thanks to all at Paines Plough, for trips to the seaside and general hand-holding. *A diolch i* Gareth Potter, *o'r diwedd.*

The Shadow of a Boy

The Shadow of a Boy was first performed at the Loft, National Theatre, London on 17 June 2002. The cast was as follows:

Luke   Rob Storr
Katie   Catrin Rhys
Nanna   Lynn Hunter
Shadow   Jo Stone-Fewings

Directed by Erica Whyman
Designed by Soutra Gilmour
Lighting by Steve Barnett
Sound by Rich Walsh

Scene One

Luke And so, it is with great regret I make my
recommendation to the Star Council: the Planet Earth is
not fit to join the Glactic League of Civilizations.
(*Deep voice.*) Agent 7272, do you recommend that the Planet
Earth be scheduled for destruction, to preserve the Glactic
Peace?
(*He considers: then, normal voice.*) No.
No. I believe there is hope for them.
They may one day be ready for Contact with the Civilized
Universe.
(*Deep voice.*) Agent 7272, your mission is complete. Prepare
for transport back to Glactic Centre /
(**Luke** *interrupts himself – normal voice.*) / No!
I'm not going back.
There is hope for the People of the Earth, but they need
help. They'll never make it alone. I'm going to stay and do –
whatever I can.
(*Deep breathing from the deep voice; then –*) Agent 7272, do you
realize you are breaking every rule in the Contact rulebook?
(*Normal voice.*)
I realize that, sir.
Just tell my mum I love her and tell my dad –
(*Deep voice.*)
Tell him what, Agent?
(*Normal voice.*) – tell him I hope one day . . . he'll be proud of
me.
(*Pause from the deep voice, then:*) I'm proud of you now, son. I'm
proud of you now . . .
(*Normal voice.*) Goodbye, sir.

Luke *salutes.*

Katie Oh my bastard Christ.
They are gonna make mincemeat of you.

Beat.

Luke Who is?

Katie   Everyone.
Everyone in the comp is.
It's bad enough being a gyppo.
But – being a spaz that talks to himself as well.

Luke   I'm not a spaz that / talks to himself.

Katie   Don't even bother 'cause I just heard you. Talking
to yourself. Like a spaz.

Beat.

Luke   I'm not a gyppo, though.

Katie   You are.

Luke   I'm not.

Katie   You are: Arthur Morris says.

Beat.

Luke   I'm not.

Katie   Oh.
All right then.
Fair do's.
(Beat.) I'll tell him you want a fight then, shall I?

Luke *looks at her.*

Katie   I'll tell him you wanna fight him for calling you a
gyppo, shall I?

Luke *doesn't answer.*

Katie   Up in the woods at the back of the base he has
them, straight after school finishes.
Straight after *comp* finishes, not after baby school finishes.
So you'll have plenty of time to get up there and shit
yourself.
You're supposed to bring somebody to hold your coat and
bag and stuff. But just – don't bring a coat is best, 'cause no
one's gonna hold yours, are they?

Luke   Don't tell Arthur I wanna fight.

Katie   Why not?

Luke (*beat*)   'Cause – I don't mind.
I don't mind him calling me a gyppo.

Katie   You don't?

Luke   The thing is /

Katie   'Cause I bloody would. I bloody would mind that.

Luke   It's just – I'm not, am I?
I'm not a gyppo, so I don't mind him calling me one.

Katie   So – I can call you anything I like.
The nastiest thing I can think of.
And it's a lie. And it's not even true.
I can say the nastiest lie I like about you, and you don't mind.

Luke *can't answer.*

Katie   So I could call you . . .
(*Searches for an insult: but changes her mind.*) Fair enough.
But if you're saying you're not a gyppo, Arthur's gonna wanna fight you for calling him a liar.

Luke   I'm not calling him a liar. I'd never do that.

Katie   So you are a gyppo then?

Luke   No.

Katie   You just called Arthur Morris a liar: I'm gonna go and tell him right now.

She spins on her heels.

Luke   No!
Don't.
Please.

Katie   Why not?

Luke   He's twelve. He's bigger than me.

Katie   What'll you give me if I don't tell him?

Luke   I –

Katie   I won't tell him – if you let me see your knickers.

Luke *hesitates:* **Katie** *holds his gaze. Finally,* **Luke** *begins to unbuckle his belt.*

Katie   Oh my God – you were gonna and all!

Luke   No I wasn't.

Katie   You bloody were, you were gonna whip your trousers down for me to see your knickers.

Luke   No!

Katie   Don't lie, you were.
I am gonna have so much fun with you.

Luke *looks at her.*

Katie   That's right.
I said: I am gonna have so much fun with you.
Do you wanna know how come?

Luke *nods.*

Katie   'Cause I'm your sister.
(*Beat.*) Go on, say something thick like, I can't be your sister
'cause you haven't got a sister. You know you want to.
(*Beat.*) I am gonna be
Your *school sister.*
And next year. In the comp.
You are going to be my little brother.
To guide and protect
And do with as I please.

Scene Two

Nanna *watches* **Luke**. *Then:*

Nanna   What is it?

Luke *looks at her.*

Nanna *looks back at him.*

Luke *looks back at her.*

Beat.

Nanna   Fine.
We'll just sit here.
And wait.
(*Beat.*) I don't mind.
(*Beat.*) Take as long as you like.

Beat.

Luke *goes to speak.*

Nanna   Finally.

Luke *hesitates.*

Nanna *looks.*

Luke   What's . . . a gyppo, Nanna?

Nanna   Why d'you want to know that?

Luke (*beat*)   I wanna know . . . all sorts of things.

Nanna   Where did you hear that word?

Luke   I just . . . heard it. (*Looks.*)

Nanna   The word . . . echoed down the hillside, did it?
And you thought to yourself: oh, I wonder what that means.

Luke   Katie Fletcher /

Nanna   Oh here we go . . . /

Luke   Katie Fletcher said Arthur Morris said I was a
gyppo.

Nanna   Did she and did he?

Luke   And – I said I wasn't.

Nanna   Even though you don't know what one is?

Beat.

Luke   Well.
I don't . . . feel like I'm a gyppo.
Do you know what I mean?

Nanna   I should hope I do.
(*Beat.*) Good instincts, you see. Good instincts you've got.
There's this whole wide world out there
And there's always more of it than you can know
But so long as you've got good instincts
You're not going to go far wrong.
(*Beat.*) So long as you've got good instincts . . .
(*She waits.*)

Luke   . . . and you remember to say your prayers.

Nanna   Well, exactly.

They smile at each other.

Nanna   The thing to keep in mind with Katie Fletcher.
(*Beat.*) It's her mother.
I remember calling at their house to collect for the harvest
festival. And she'd –
– been to the bakers *and bought a sponge.*
A Victoria sponge.
I said to her, Mrs Fletcher – because I think she still is a
Mrs, in the eyes of the law at least – Mrs Fletcher, there's no
need to go to the bakers for sponge. You should've said, I'd
have given you my recipe for bara brith.
Oh no, she says, I'm a dead loss at baking. Nonsense, I say
to her, bara brith, it's the simplest thing you could imagine
and my recipe – well, my grandmother's recipe, to be exact
– my recipe is *simpler still.*
Even so, she goes, I'm sure I'd manage to make a mess of it
somehow.
Well, I said to her. I can hardly credit it.
A woman like yourself. A woman with education.
And oh, she goes, oh I'm afraid an education doesn't
guarantee expertise in the kitchen –
– well there's a thing, I tell her: a woman like yourself who
can't even make a bara brith for the harvest festival –

– and *still* you think you know better than the God that
made the sun and the sky and the stars and you won't send
little Katie to Sunday School.
(*Beat.*) That's what you're contending with.
When you contend with the Fletchers.
So my advice is just: steer clear.

Luke *is still worried.*

Nanna   What, lovely?

Luke   But Nanna –
– I still don't know –
What is a gyppo, then?

Nanna   Gyppo is a word that ignorant people – like Katie
Fletcher – call gypsies, or anyone who's a bit common, and
looks like they might steal clothes off the line.

Luke   So I am a gyppo, aren't I?

Nanna *looks.*

Luke   'Cause gypsies live in caravans, don't they.
And –
– I used to live in a caravan.

Nanna (*beat*)   You did.
You did, but you don't now.
(*Beat.*) Just – steer clear of her sort, is my advice.

Beat.

Luke   Well good.
I will steer clear.
I don't like her.

Nanna   It's not her fault, mind.

Luke   No, but I'm glad.
'Cause she was saying.

Nanna *looks.*

Luke   She was saying.

Nanna   *What*, lovely?

Luke   She was saying all this stuff about.
You know.
Her being my sister.
Like my school sister.
And she says I'm supposed to go round hers and have tea so
she can tell me all about the comp, and then on the first day
of school she's gotta sit with me on the bus and take me to
my class and all that.
But I'm glad.
I'm glad I've gotta steer clear.
'Cause I don't wanna go round hers for tea and sit next to
her on the bus –

Nanna   – Luke.

Luke *looks.*

Nanna   Why didn't you say straight off?

Luke   First things first you always say.
Or I've heard you say it sometimes.
And first, I wanted to know what a gyppo was and if I am
one.

Nanna   I'm sure you did.
But you also wanted –
– you are sly as a snake.

Beat.

Luke   No.

Nanna   Luke –

Luke   Nanna –

Beat.

Luke   You said steer clear /

Nanna   I know.
(*Beat.*) It wouldn't be very nice if you got lost on your first
day, would it.

Luke *says nothing.*

Nanna Think what the teachers would say if you got lost and you were late on your very first day.

Luke *says nothing.*

Nanna That wouldn't be a very good start, would it.

Luke You said.
You said Katie was a bad apple.

Nanna Well, she is, but I'm not telling you to pick up her bad habits /

Luke And you said her mum was a right slack Alice.

Nanna I said no such thing.

Luke You did.
You did. You said it to Mrs Hughes.
You didn't say it, you spelled it out.
But I'm not five. I'm ten.
(*Beat.*) We were buying spuds at Jack Williams.
You talked for ages. You said we were going straight to the paper shop for my comic but then we popped into Jack Williams for spuds and there was / Mrs Hughes

Nanna You –
– shouldn't have been listening.

Luke I wasn't listening.
I just – heard.

Nanna *looks at him.*

Luke She can't cook or anything.
I'll get food poisoning if I go for tea at theirs.
I'll die.

Nanna There must be things you're wondering about the grammar school, things I don't know about.

Luke There's not. There's nothing.
(*Beat.*) And it's a comprehensive, not a grammar school.

Nanna   Well –
– well, there you go, don't you?
I don't even properly know what it's called.

Beat.

Luke   Nanna.
I don't want to.

Nanna *looks at him.*

Scene Three

Luke   My nanna says I can't come over for tea on
Sunday, 'cause I have to go to Sunday School.

Katie   My mum says Sunday school's a load of rubbish,
but she understands how your nan would want a few hours'
peace from your whining over the weekend.

Beat.

Luke   So Nanna thought Saturday –

Katie   – Saturday's no good, mum's working Saturday –

Luke   – which is why Nanna thought you could come
over to ours for tea on Saturday.
(*Beat.*) There's rhubarb coming up in the garden. We're
having proper home-baked rhubarb crumble.

Katie   I don't like proper home-baked rhubarb crumble.

Luke   How would you know? Your mum can't bake
nothing.

Beat.

Katie   D'you know what my mum says about your nan?

Luke   I don't care what any slack Alice says.

Beat.

Katie   She says your nanna
Has got a heart of gold.
(*Beat*). Which is what she always says when she thinks
someone's a mad old cow.

Beat.

Luke   I don't want you to come to ours.
Nanna says /

Katie   I'm sure you don't.
I wouldn't want anyone to come to mine if I lived in a dump
like yours.
But it'll be great.
I'll be able to see all your teddy bears, and dolls.
And find out how bad your house smells.
They usually smell.
Houses with old people living in them.
'Cause old people are nearly dead.
And dead things usually smell.
They usually smell like /
/ you're not going to cry, are you, Lukey?

Luke   No.

Katie   No?

Luke   I haven't got teddy bears and the house doesn't
smell.

Katie   Oh, and so you don't mind.
'Cause you don't mind people saying things that aren't true.

Luke *says nothing.*

Katie   What if I said something that is true, then?
(*Beat.*) What if I said –
– little orphan boy.
Haven't got no mummy.
Haven't got no dad.
It's one thing just having no mum. Or just having no dad. I
haven't got a dad. Loads of people haven't got a dad.
But having no mum *and* having no dad.

(*Beat.*) Talks to himself 'cause he hasn't got a mum or a dad
to talk to.
Just a batty old nan.
Haven't got no mum.
Haven't got no dad.
That's – what they'll all be singing.
When you get on the bus the first day at school.
Here's the little freakboy
Who lives with his batty old nan.
(*Beat.*) They'll be saying – what was the last thing that went
through Luke's dad's head?
Luke's *mum*.
(*Beat.*) And of course you'd crash your car.
Of course you would
If your son was a freak
Just to get some peace from his bloody whining.
(*Beat.*) Of course you'd crash your car.
Rather than go to parents' evening and schoolplay and
sportsday and have to tell everyone yes, that's him, that's our
son freakboy Luke blabbering away to himself in the corner.
(*Beat.*) You gonna cry now, Lukey?

Beat.

Luke   No.

Beat.
Katie *goes to say something else.*
She stops herself.
Comes closer to **Luke** *and inspects him*
She stares at him for a long time.

Luke (*looks at her, then*)   I'm not gonna cry.
'Cause I haven't got nothing to cry about.
(*Beat.*) I'm going now.

Beat.

Katie   Luke.

Beat.

Katie   If someone.
At the comp, no one does stuff like showing their knickers,
right. That's just for baby school.
If someone asks you to show them your knickers, you do
this –

*She hooks the top of her pants with her middle finger and pulls them out
from her jeans: then she lets them slip back into her jeans, and presents
her finger.*

Katie   – and you tell them to spin, all right?

Beat.

Katie   Well, go on then. Show me.

Beat.
Luke *doesn't move.*

Katie   Don't say I didn't try to help you, all right?

Luke *turns to go.*
He pauses.

Luke   Katie?

Katie *looks.*

He gives her the finger.

Luke   Spin on that.

Scene Four

Nanna (*beat*)   You can say now, or I'll just have to sit here.
(*She waits for him to speak. He doesn't.*) If I don't get to bed soon,
I'm going to be awfully bad-tempered in the morning, and I
won't be in the mood to make porridge, and we'll end up
having the brussel sprouts from supper for breakfast /

Luke   Katie was teasing me.

Nanna   What about, lovely?

Luke *doesn't answer.*

Nanna *holds his gaze.*

Luke   She was trying to make me cry.

Nanna   You know what you have to do when someone
says nasty things to try and upset you. You just have to
think: are any of these things true?
And you'll find they're not true of you, but they might well
be true of the person who's teasing you /

Luke   She –

Nanna *pulls up.*

Luke   She wasn't saying nasty things that aren't true.
She was trying to make me cry.

Nanna (*beat*)   And did you?

Luke *shakes his head.*

Nanna   Good lad.

She gets quickly up.

Luke   Nanna?

Nanna *waits.*

Luke (*beat*)   Could you.
Can I have a story?

Nanna *doesn't answer.*

Luke   Nanna?

Nanna   Don't you think you're a bit old for stories?
Wouldn't you rather read your comics?

Luke (*beat*)   S'pose.

Nanna *makes to go.*

Luke   Nanna.

Nanna *waits.*

Luke   I didn't cry.

Nanna   'Cause you're a good lad.

Luke   Katie asked me why I didn't cry.

Beat.

Can I have the story, Nanna?

Beat.

Nanna *turns, sits down again.*

Nanna (*beat*)   You'd stayed over with me, 'cause mummy and daddy were working late, building your house so you wouldn't have to live in the caravan.
When I woke it was raining, just a drizzle, but enough for the sunlight to catch and flicker in the drops, enough that there were tiny rainbows wherever you looked.
The light must've woken you.
Not the rain. The rain was too soft. It must've been the light.
(*Beat.*) I opened my eyes.
I breathed in.
I sat up.
And all round me were snowdrops.
Still damp from the garden. That fresh smell of the morning filling my bedroom.
(*Beat.*) The light had woken you.
The snowdrops had come up overnight and you'd put on your raincoat and your wellies and gone out into the garden and picked them.
And then laid them out around me, while I was still asleep.
(*Beat.*) Luke.

Luke   I was six, wasn't I.

Nanna   Yes, you were.
Luke –

Luke   I was just six, and I'd gone out and picked the snowdrops and that's how you knew it was –

Nanna (*beat*)   A special day.

Luke   A very special day.

Nanna (*beat*)   Your daddy was working for Mr Badham.
And your mummy was working at the Cartwheel.
And even when he was working very very late
Your daddy would stop by and look in on you.
You'd always try and stay awake.
You'd lie on your belly, propped on your elbows, your
fingers pushing your eyelids up so you wouldn't fall asleep.
You always did fall asleep in the end.
But your daddy stopped by and checked on you anyway.
(*Beat.*) The house was almost finished.
Your daddy had picked up your mum.
And God must've seen your house and seen how well your
daddy had built it.
And He thought He needed someone to build houses in
Heaven.
Because sometimes God picks people for special jobs.

Luke   Like the shepherds on the hillside?

Nanna   Like the shepherds on the hillside, that He sent to
greet the Lord Jesus.
(*Beat.*) Only the very best people.
And you're very lucky your dad was picked for such a
special job.

Luke   I know.

Nanna   And your mummy had to go with your dad –

Luke   – because how could dad build houses without
mummy to help him?

Nanna   Exactly.

Luke   And I never cried.
I never cried once.

Nanna   Not once.

Luke   And why not?
Why didn't I cry?

Nanna (*beat*)   What is there to cry about, when your mummy and daddy are picked to do the Lord's work?

Luke   Nothing.

Nanna   Nothing.
(*Beat.*) I looked out over the garden and there wasn't a single snowdrop to be seen. I thought you'd picked them all – but you'd left one last patch: you'd hidden them.
You'd put a bucket over them to keep them safe. You didn't realize they needed the rain and the sun, so they'd grow up big and strong.

Luke   I know now, though.

Nanna   Yes, you do.

Luke   But Nanna –

Nanna *waits.*

Luke   – if mum had to go with dad, how come –

Nanna   Luke, please.

Luke   It's just, I don't quite understand /

Nanna *draws back from him: he dries up.*

Luke (*beat*)   Nanna –

Nanna (*turns back to him*)   – What now, lovely?

Beat.

Shadow   Luke.

Luke *doesn't respond.*

Nanna   Little man?

Shadow   Luke.

Nanna   It's better out than in, whatever it is.

Shadow   Luke.
You know why you had to stay behind.
Don't you.

Luke *looks at him.*

Shadow   Don't you.

Luke *doesn't answer.*

Shadow   You had to stay, 'cause you had a mission.
Right?
(*Beat.*)   Am I right?
(*Beat.*) Shadow to Luke, are you reading me, Luke?

Luke *barely nods.*

Shadow   At *last*.

Nanna   What is it, lovely?

Shadow   Could you get rid of her? We've got loads to do
and really – not that much time at all.

Luke (*beat*)   Nothing, Nanna.
I was just –

Nanna *looks at him.*

Luke   Can I read my comics for a bit, Nanna?

Nanna   It's already / well past your bed time.

Shadow   / I wonder what'd happen
If you were to look really really sad, right now.
Go on, give us a pout.

Luke *does so.*

Nanna (*beat*)   All right then. Just for a little while.

Luke   Thank you, Nanna.

Nanna *kisses him: leaves.*

Shadow (*watches her go, then*)   Star Cadet Luke: welcome to
the team.

Scene Five

Shadow's *weighed down with bits of kit dangling from straps and harnesses: in particular, he's hulking round a portable reel-to-reel tape recorder with a microphone dangling from it, and an early eighties model Polaroid. He snaps things occasionally, or inspects them with a plastic* Star Trek-*style tricorder.*

Shadow   And you use these for . . . what?

Luke   They're just flowers.

Shadow   Varieties of powderized wheat grain used in the making of bread?

Luke   They just look nice. And smell nice.

Shadow *sniffs sceptically.*

Shadow   Perhaps – to deeply primitive sense organs.

Shadow *fiddles with his Polaroid. It doesn't seem to be working.*

Shadow   Oh, what now?

Luke   What's wrong?

Shadow   The . . .

Luke   Holographic scanner?

Shadow   The holographic scanner's playing up again.

He gives up on the Polaroid.

Luke   Was it like a rocket you came in? Or a saucer?

Shadow   Nothing like that. I didn't come in a *thing*.

Luke   They beamed you down?

Shadow   You might call it that. If you didn't know what you were talking about, at all.

Shadow *shakes himself down.*

Luke   What?

Shadow This *body*. It's like it thinks there's only four dimensions in the universe.

Luke Aren't there?

Shadow *looks at him.*

Luke You'll need the names of them. The flowers.

Shadow Really?

Luke Of course.

Shadow All right. If we must . . .

Luke This is a bluebell, and this is a / primrose

Shadow Hold on, hold on.

He struggles with the tape machine. **Luke** *watches.* **Shadow** *finally switches the tape on and holds the mike at* **Luke**.

Shadow Okay.

Luke Right, so this is a bluebell, and this is a primrose, and this is forget-me-not, and these . . . these are just kinds of grasses. Nanna's got a book, I can look them up and find out exactly what kinds later /

Shadow Can't I say they're just grass?

Luke You can if you don't mind not doing your job properly.

Beat.

Shadow We'll get the book. And what's this?

Luke A foxglove.

Shadow A glove for foxes? How does that work? How's a fox get that on his / paw?

Luke No, that's just the name of it. It's not really a glove. And – don't touch them. They're poisonous. To humans, anyway.

Shadow I'll keep that in mind.

Luke   And these are – ow!

Shadow   What?

Luke *rubs his hand.*

Luke   A stinging nettle.

Shadow   And what's that do?

Luke   Well it stings, doesn't it.

Shadow   Are you . . . gonna cry?

Luke   No.

Shadow   Does stinging not hurt then?
I thought stinging was a thing that hurt.
Does it not? Can you explain that to me somehow?

Luke   I'm not gonna cry.

Shadow (*beat*)   It's not very kind, is it, leaving stuff like
that around the place? Stuff that poisons you, stuff that
stings you. I'm not sure he's all you crack him up to be . . .

Luke *searches; finds what he's looking for.*

Luke   See this?
It's a dock leaf. It takes away the sting of the nettle thief.
And wherever you find stinging nettles, you find dock leaves
growing just by to make you better.

Beat.

Shadow   So . . . when do I get to meet him, then?

Luke   You can't *meet* Him.

Shadow   But it's the first thing I'm supposed to do. Hit
the ground, preferably running, collar some natives and
demand they take me to their leader, who you claim to be
this – (*He consults a notebook.*) – 'God' bloke.

Luke   Yeah, but you can't just meet Him.

Shadow   So what, do I . . . make an appointment?

Luke   No it's not like that, it's . . . You can't see Him, is the thing. You just know He's here.

Shadow   You just know.

Luke   You look around, and you just know.

Shadow   You look around at the stinging nettles and poison flowers?

Luke   You look around at the dock leaves and the pretty flowers.

Beat.

Shadow   Has he got a deputy or something I could talk to?

Luke   *No!*
Well, He's got vicars, and things.
I mean, there's my Nanna –

Nanna   Luke?

Luke   – but she's not really a deputy or anything. Not officially, like.

Nanna *comes into the garden.*

Nanna   Come in and wash your hands for tea.

Luke *pouts.*

Nanna   And then you can fetch the cheese and the salmon spread from the pantry.

Luke *pouts even more.*

Nanna   Fish is good for you, Luke.

Luke   Be better for you if it didn't have all bones in it.

Nanna   There's no bones in salmon spread.
Besides which, the Lord only puts bones in fishes so you'll take time over your food, instead of wolfing it down like a . . .

Luke   . . . wolf?

Nanna (*smiling*)   Just get in here and wash your hands, little man.

Nanna *leaves.*

Shadow's *staring at* **Luke**, *confused.*

Luke   What now?

Shadow   Just remind me again: fish?

Luke   What good are you?

Shadow   Well . . . there's a lot to take in, isn't there.

Luke   Okay. Fishes are the things that live in the water –

Shadow   – oh yeah, and if you take them out of the water and put them on the land where we are, they die. (*Stares at him, then:*) They're things from the river?

Luke   Yeah.

Shadow   Those blue things you collect, the ones on your shelf?

Luke (*thinks; then*)   No! You idiot, those are bottles, mun.

Shadow   But you found them in the river /

Luke   Those are old bottles that people have thrown away, they're not living things.

Shadow   They're not living now, but how do you know they weren't alive before you pulled them out of the water?

Beat.

Luke   You are . . . the worst person I can think of for this job.

Shadow   Feeling guilty now, 'cause of all those bottles you killed /

Luke   You can't kill bottles, right? They're just . . . things. That people make. Fishes are *living* things. That God makes. And – they're just not the same . . . *kind* of thing.

Beat.

Though . . . once, I found a bottle in the river, and picked it up – and there was a fish inside it.

Shadow   What'd'you do?

Luke   I took it home. Put it on my shelf.

Shadow   And what happened?

Luke   The fish died.
Not straight away, like, but – after an hour or two.

Beat.

Shadow   So . . . do the fishes *live* in the bottles?

Luke   I don't know.
Maybe.
Anyway, there's no fish in the river any more.

Shadow   Where've they gone?

Luke   Uh . . . to the sea. I think.

Shadow   Maybe they haven't gone anywhere. Maybe it's part of the fish lifecycle, that after they've been fishes for a while they settle down and transform into bottles. Maybe the bottle is like a fish-chrysalis, and the fishes go into them for a bit and then come out as . . . seagulls. Or kingfishers. Or . . . butterflies.

Luke   I don't think so . . .

Shadow   And if the fishes do live in bottles, maybe that's why there's none in the river any more. 'Cause maybe collecting all the bottles from the river, you've . . . you've taken all the fishes' houses. And now they're just . . . wandering round the river, with nowhere to go, looking for their houses but they can't find them 'cause Luke has nicked them all and put them on his shelf. Did you ever think of that?

Beat.
Katie *approaches.*

Luke   Are you gonna be here long?

Shadow   Till my mission is completed. Or I die in the attempt.

Katie   All right, freakboy.

Luke (*beat*)   I wasn't talking to myself.

Katie   No. Well.
We both know you were.
(*Beat.*) Let's get this over with, shall we.

Katie *strides off.*

Shadow   What – was that?

Luke   That was – a girl.

Shadow   And what the hell are they?

Luke   They are –
– they're the same kind of thing as Nanna.

Shadow   Really?
'Cause that thing –

Luke   Katie Fletcher –

Shadow   – that Katie Fletcher didn't look anything like Nanna.

Luke   Katie's like eleven, and Nanna's . . . loads older than that.

Shadow   So they're at different stages of the lifecycle, are they?

Luke   . . . yeah . . .

Shadow   . . . and is there a chrysalis involved? Does a Katie go into a something and come out all different?

Luke (*beat*)   Yes.
Yes, there is.
There's a thing called *getting married*.
A Katie goes into that.
And when she's married she gets all wrinkly and old.
And she comes out – a Nanna.

Scene Six

Shadow   And pepper is?

Luke   It's just . . . to make food taste nice.

Shadow   Eating is a something we do so the body doesn't run out of energy.

Luke   I suppose . . . but you can make it taste nice as well.

Beat.

Shadow   And that's what all this . . . 'cookery' is about?

Luke   Yeah. There are people called chefs and that's all they do, is cook things really really well. And you go to their restaurants and dress up and have white wine or a pint of beer. And you have prawn cocktail to start, then chicken in a basket or spaghetti bolognese, and black forest gateau for sweet.

Shadow   It's the simplest thing, taking on fuel. Why d'you have to make so fussy?

Luke   It's not fussy, it's good. Things don't have to be boring all the time.

Nanna (*coming in*)   Apparently at Katie's house they don't consider it important to wash hands before a meal.
I've shown her the sink and the soap and how the taps work. (*Beat.*) We'll just have to hope for the best.

Shadow   No, things don't *have* to be boring. They just are on this planet.

Luke   Don't moan 'cause you don't like it /

Shadow   Can you fly? 'Cause you can where I come from. Because we have transcended the brute corporeal existence you suffer in this dump.

Nanna   And I don't want to find any salmon spread sandwiches smeared across the bottom of the table, all right? 'Cause if I do, I'll scrape them off and fry them up and you'll be having them for supper.

Luke   I'll eat them properly this time, Nanna.

Shadow   Hold on –
– are you saying –
– all that fuss and you don't even like the stuff?

Luke   I don't like salmon spread sandwiches, no.

Shadow   So why d'you bother eating them?

Luke   'Cause Nanna says so.

Shadow   Chuck them to me, I'll dump them in the stream. Back where they belong.

Luke   No.

Shadow   She'll never find out.

Luke   That's not the point. She made it for me, and she said I got to eat it so /

Shadow   But you don't like it /

Luke   It's probably good for me.

Shadow   How can it be good for you if you hate it. That's rubbish.

Luke   I can see why they send you on all the really dangerous missions.

Shadow *looks at him.*

Luke (*beat*)   They send you on the dangerous missions 'cause you're the bravest and the best.

Shadow   I was only trying help you out.

Luke   I know /

Shadow   Just trying to help a mate, like.

Luke   I know /

Shadow   But if you don't want my help . . .

Luke   I do, though.

Shadow   Do you?

Luke *nods.*

Shadow   You sure?

Luke   Yes.

Beat.
In the distance, a siren.

Shadow   What's that then?

Beat.

Luke   Don't know.

Shadow   You've never heard it before.

Luke   I've –
– heard it before.
Just . . .

Shadow   You weren't really listening.

Luke   No.

Shadow   So. Now you are.
What is it?

Luke   I don't know.

Shadow   How you gonna find out?

Luke *looks at him.*

Shadow   Go on.

Beat.

Luke   Nanna?

Nanna   Mmmm?

Luke   What's that noise, Nanna?

Nanna   Just the pans rattling, lovely.

Luke   No, Nanna, like that wailing noise –

He does an impression of the siren.

Nanna   Why d'you want to know that, little man?

Luke *looks to* **Shadow**.
Shadow *whispers in his ear.*

Luke   'Cause . . . Katie said it was a signal for all the big
kids at the comp, to stuff all the first years' heads down the
toilet and flush it.

Nanna *relaxes.*

Nanna   It's a horn from the cheese factory in Whitland. It
tells all the workers their shift is over.

Shadow*'s listening to this carefully – he looks to* **Luke***: Is this the
truth?* **Luke** *picks up his glance.*

Luke   Really?

Nanna   Yes.

Luke   In Whitland? And the noise carries all the way to
us?

Nanna   It has to be loud, lovely, so the workers can hear it
over the machinery.

Luke *glances to* **Shadow;** **Shadow** *shrugs.*

Luke   Fair enough, then.

Katie *enters.*

Nanna   Sit yourself down, Katie.
Would you like tea or coffee?

Katie   Tea.

Nanna   Good. Coffee, as we know, is the very nectar of
the devil himself.

Nanna *holds* **Katie***'s gaze.*

Luke   Nanna thinks she's funny.

Nanna *cracks a smile.*

Nanna   Luke?

Luke *looks to* **Katie***, then closes his eyes and clasps his hands.*
Nanna *stares at* **Katie** *until she follows suit.*

Luke   Lord, we thank you for what we're about to receive,
and pray that you bless us and preserve us. Amen.

Nanna   Amen.

Katie   A-men.

Shadow*'s peering at* **Katie***, distracting* **Luke***.*

Nanna   So, Katie, Luke's very eager to hear all about the
comprehensive school. Aren't you, Luke?

Luke   Yes, Nanna.

Katie   What'd you wanna know?

Luke   Dunno. Anything, I s'pose.

Katie   All right then . . . Well . . . whatever you do, don't
sit anywhere in the back four rows on the bus, or the sixth-
formers'll kick you in.

Luke*'s getting alarmed 'cause* **Shadow** *has pulled out his Polaroid
and is taking snaps of* **Katie***.*

Luke   O-kay . . .

Katie   And behind the metalwork block, there's some
psycho kids have got their den there, and you see them

going there every break and sniffing superglue and they
come out with their eyes all like this – (*She flicks her eyes up into
her head, so only the whites show.*) and all gunk around their
mouths /

Nanna   Would you like some jam on your bread, Katie?
I've got blackberry, and raspberry, and apricot. I made it
myself, from the garden.

Katie   Have you got any strawberry?

Nanna (*beat*)   We have, but it's only rubbish from the
shop, there's no proper fruit in it /

Katie   I'd much prefer strawberry, if that's all right with
you.

Nanna *gets up and ferrets.*
Shadow *leans right in front of* **Katie** *to take a picture of her face.*
Luke *struggles not to look at him.*

Luke (*to* **Shadow**)   Will you get lost?

Shadow   All right, all right.

Shadow *scuttles away.* **Luke** *smiles nervily at* **Katie**.
Katie *stares back at him.*
Luke's *smile dies.*
Satisfied, **Katie** *takes a mouthful of tea.*

Katie   God!

Nanna *spins round.*

Nanna   What?

Katie   Nothing. The tea's just really weak, is all.

Nanna   You've not burned yourself?

Katie *shakes her head.*

Nanna   Good. Here's your jam.

Katie *takes the jam without saying thank you, opens it up and starts
ladling huge lumps of it on to her bread.*

Nanna *watches for a moment as* **Katie** *stuffs the jam-loaded bread into her mouth.* **Katie** *smiles at her.* **Nanna** *can take no more.*

Nanna   And I'd thank you not to use that sort of language while you're in my home.

Katie   I didn't say nothing.

Nanna   You blasphemed.

Katie *looks to* **Luke** *in bewilderment.*

Luke   You said (*He mouths.*) 'God'.

Katie   'God' isn't swearing. It *isn't*.

Nanna   It's not a rude word, no.

Katie   So what'd I do?

Beat.

I didn't do nothing, did I?

Beat.

Nanna   You know, Katie, just the other day, Luke had a jam sandwich, and he stuffed it in his mouth and dropped crumbs everywhere, and got jam all over his chops, and I said to him, 'Luke, you're as bad as Katie Fletcher.'

Katie *becomes horribly aware she's got jam on her mouth.*

Nanna   – and we had a little laugh about it. But I'd never say such a thing while you were here – that'd be rude. 'Cause that might well upset you, mightn't it.

Katie   Yes. It might well.

Nanna   And God is everywhere. So whenever you use the Lord's name to mean something bad, then you're going to upset Him.

Beat.

Katie   I think . . . I've had enough to eat now.

Beat.

Nanna   You don't want any rhubarb crumble?

Katie   No, thank you.

Nanna   But you've hardly had a thing /

Katie   I'm full, thank you very much.

Beat.

I'd like to go home now, please.

Nanna   You can't go home yet.
Your mother won't be back for another two hours.

Katie *says nothing.*

Shadow   You can't let her go yet. I've barely filled half a
. . . databank.

Luke   What am I supposed to do?

Shadow   You could – think of something?

Luke (*flusters, then*)   But you haven't seen my . . . collection
of old bottles, yet. From the river /

Katie   Oh well. That would be lovely. I'd love to see your
collection of old bottles, please Luke. And they're from the
river? That sounds . . . fascinating.

Beat.

Nanna   Well, in that case, you're both excused.

They get up and go to leave. **Luke** *leads the way.*
As **Katie**'s *about to leave the room:*

Nanna   Katie.

Katie *stops.*

Nanna   If you do want something else to eat /

Katie   I'm sure I'll be fine, thank you very much, Mrs
Evans.

Scene Seven

Luke   These are the bottles.

Katie   Oh.

Katie   I don't know how you stick it.
(*Beat.*) All that God crap all the time.

She hovers at an immense, vast, huge pile of comics.

You like comics, do you?

Luke   A bit.

Katie   A bit?
My mum doesn't believe in comics. She says they promote neo-Fascist militarism.

Shadow *looks questioningly to* **Luke**. **Luke** *picks up the look.*

Luke   What's that mean?

Katie   They make boys think it's cool to shoot people.

Luke   Oh, I don't like them for the war stories.

Katie   No?

Luke   I like the – this is my favourite, 'Shadow of the Stars'. It's about this kid who – there's this thing, the Glactic League and they survey all the planets and decide if they're ready to join the League, and the Star Council send down this little alien called Shadow, and his mission is –

Shadow *stands to mock-attention, joins sarcastically in with* **Luke**:

Shadow/Luke   – 'to know and comprehend the people of the Earth, without prejudice or favour, to understand their virtues and their flaws, and to judge whether the Earth is ready to join the Glactic League of Civilizations'.

Shadow *salutes, goes back to peering at* **Katie**.

Shadow   And what fantastic mission it's turning out to be . . .

Luke   – and no one on Earth can see Shadow except this one boy, and the boy has to show Shadow around, and explain stuff on Earth to him. I've got the whole story. It starts in *Hawk* 34, the January 12th, 1978 issue, and ends in *Hawk* 228, the Christmas issue in 1982.

Katie   And . . . what happens?

Luke   Well . . .
. . . loads of things.
But in the end, Shadow decides that the Earth isn't ready to join the rest of Glactic civilization –

Katie   – which any sane person can see in ten seconds –

Shadow   I like . . . girls' hair. Girls' hair is better than boys' hair.

Luke   – but from learning about us, he decides that Glactic civilization is really boring, and so he wants to stay here.

Katie   What a rem.

Shadow *looks at her.*

Katie   So, is this what you do?

Luke   What I . . . do?

Katie   You just read bollocks like that, and go to Sunday school?

Luke   It's not . . .

Katie   It's not what?

Luke   It's not . . .
(*Beat.*) I think they're good, is all. I think it's a good story.

Katie   Why won't you say 'bollocks'?

Luke *doesn't answer.*

Beat.

Katie   I might sod off, I reckon . . .

Shadow *jabs* **Luke** *in the ribs.*

Luke   Do you want to . . . play a game?

Katie   What sort of game?

Luke   Uh . . . I've got Operation, and Ker-plunk, and Risk /

Katie   What about Nervous?

Luke (*beat*)   Okay.

Katie   Tops. Come on then.

Luke   What'm I supposed to do?

Katie   You just come and sit down by me.
And what we do is, I put my hand on your knee –
– and you've gotta say if it makes you nervous.
Does it?

Luke (*beat*)   No.

Katie   So then I move my hand up a bit –
Does that make you nervous?

Luke   . . . No.

Katie   What about that /

Luke   Yes!

Katie *sniggers at him.*

Luke   That's a useless game.

Katie   And now you've got to do it to me.

Luke *hesitates.*

Katie   Or, I can tell everyone in comp you're a chicken . . .

Luke   All right, all right.

He complies.
She's wearing a skirt that falls a couple of inches above the knee when she sits.

Luke Nervous?

Katie No.

Luke *moves his hand a quarter of an inch up her leg.*

Luke Nervous?

Katie No.

Another quarter of an inch.

Luke Ner/vous?

Katie No.

Another quarter of an inch.

Luke Nervous?

Katie Not even slightly.

Luke'*s hand reaches the hem of her skirt. He slides his hand up another quarter of an inch – but over her skirt.*

Luke Nerv/ous?

Katie You're supposed to put your hand under my skirt.

Luke *stares at her for a second.*

Luke I don't wanna play this any more.

Katie You are *so* dead when you get to the comp.

Luke I don't care.

Katie But, you will.

She goes over to a window.

Luke What're you doing?

Katie Leaving. I reckon I can get on to your porch from here.

Shadow *looks to* **Luke**.

Luke Your mum's not home yet.

Katie   Aw, that's right, I'd better sit round here for two hours with you boring me shitless then, hadn't I.

Shadow *looks carefully at* **Katie**, *then whispers to* **Luke**.

Luke   I'll tell you a secret if you stay.

Katie   Oh yeah?

Luke *nods*.

Katie   Do you even know any good secrets?

Luke   This one's really good.

Katie *sits down on the bed*.

Katie   Tell away, then.

Luke   If you get in the river where it comes through our garden, and walk down it back towards the village, you come to the hedge between Mr Scale's farm and Mr Beynon's farm. And that hedge – isn't a hedge. It's a stream, but it's all so overgrown it looks like a hedge.

Katie   That better not be it.

Luke   That's not even half of it. 'Cause if you walk up this stream, it's like crawling through the jungle, and you get your face scrammed to bits, but after you've got your face scrammed to bits you come out by this old bridge, on the backroad to Robinson Wathen.
When you're driving down the backroad, you've got to be lucky 'cause it's two and a half miles and only one ditch to overtake in, so if you meet someone coming the other way, you're in trouble. You've gotta reverse all the way back to where you came from.
But usually you don't meet anyone, 'cause no one knows about it, just people from the valley who cut through. And the only other people who go on that road are Arthur Morris, and Paul Barclay, and Davy Matthews and all those kids from the comp. They go down there and hang round on the bridge, and they chuck stuff in the stream, and try to fish with these little rods they made out of sticks.

And when they're sitting there pretending to fish . . . they talk about girls.
They talk about what girls they like in the comp.
Paul Barclay likes Joanne Moore, and Davy Matthews likes Mary Francis. Arthur Morris liked Gaynor Price, but now he likes Anna Price. Cause, he says, Anna isn't so tight. And I know, because I go there, after school.
And . . . I just sit. There's a couple of big rocks under there sticking out of the water and I get there and sit with the fishes and the moss and the spiders, and I hear . . . everything.

Katie   That is a cool secret.

Luke   Yeah.

Katie   That is a fucking cool secret.

Luke *recoils a little at the oath.*

Katie   Have you ever said a swear word in your life?

Luke   Yeah.

Katie   Say 'fuck' then.

Luke *says nothing.*

Katie   Or 'bastard'.

Luke *says nothing.*

Katie   Or at least 'shit'.

Beat.

Katie   Why're you scared of saying stuff like that?

Luke   I'm not scared. I just . . . don't want to.

Katie   Is it 'cause it upsets your nanna?

Luke   Nuh.

Katie   Is it 'cause . . . it upsets God? Do you think you'll burn in hell if you say a swear word?

Shadow   Is that true? Is that what he does to you?

Luke *(to both)*   No!

Shadow   What a bastard . . .

Katie   You are scared, aren't you?

Luke   No! I just don't wanna say them words, all right? I'd say them if I blummin well wanted to.

Katie   You 'blummin well' would, would you?

Luke   Yeah.

Katie *stares at him.*

Kate   Do you wanna know a secret, Luke?

Luke *doesn't know; glances to* **Shadow***.*

Luke   What sort of secret?

Katie   The biggest secret in the world.

Luke   S'pose.

Katie   Are you sure? 'Cause you can't forget it once you know.

Beat.

Luke   Go on then.

Katie   Say 'shit'.

Luke   You didn't say I / had to –

Katie   Say 'shit' if you want to know the biggest secret in the whole wide world.

Luke   No.

Shadow   Luke!

Luke   No.

Shadow   Oh right, I'll just turn up at Glactic Centre and say 'oh yeah, there's this really big secret on Earth –

Katie Just once, Luke.

Shadow – but I never quite managed to find it out.
Sorry, like.'

Katie Did you know, Luke, 'shit' is Welsh for 'how'. So
you could make the sound, but just be saying 'how' in
Welsh.

Shadow I think that's actually true.
(*Beat.*) It was in the Planetary Notes.

Katie So it wouldn't really be swearing.

Beat.

Luke Okay then . . .
Shit.

Katie I can't believe you swore.

Luke It wasn't swearing, it was Welsh.

Katie You don't speak Welsh.

Luke No, but – I was saying 'how' in Welsh.

Katie You said 'shit'. You're gonna burn in hell.

Luke *opens the window.*

Luke You can go now, if you want.

Katie Don't you want to know the secret?

Beat.

Luke All right then.

Beat. **Katie** *smiles*

Katie They're going to kill us all.

Luke *looks.*

Katie They're gonna fry us. With great big bombs. And
even one bomb is enough to destroy the Earth, and they've

got hundreds and millions of them. And they're gonna blow
us up.

Beat.

Luke   Why?

Katie   Nobody knows.

Luke   When?

Katie   They won't say. There'll just be a warning. It'll be
on the telly. We'll get three minutes and then – boom.
That's the end of everything.

Luke   But . . . we haven't got a telly.

Katie   You won't even get a warning then.

Luke   But that's / not fair.

Katie   You'll just be there one day having your tea and –
there'll be this light and the house will fall down and you
and your nanna'll be blown to bits.
(*Beat.*) But then again – do you hear the siren at nights
sometimes?

Luke *nods.*

Katie   Do you know what it is?

Luke *shakes his head.*

Katie   It's from the base. It's where all the Americans
keep their bombs. And that's their siren to say that they've
got to blow them all up. So when you hear that, you know –
boom. You're gonna get it.

Luke   But – I hear that every night, nearly.

Katie   They've got to test to make sure it's working
properly.

Luke   So how do you know if they're testing it or if it's . . .
for real?

Katie   If you hear it and three minutes later you're not blown to bits, then you know they were just testing it out.

Silence.

Fucking cool secret, huh?

Luke *nods.*

Scene Eight

Shadow *enters, stands right behind* **Luke** *with the Polaroid. He waits for* **Luke** *to turn round and snaps as he does so.* **Luke** *jumps.*

Shadow   Bit –
– jumpy, Luke?

Luke   'Course I am, with you creeping up behind me.

Shadow   Sorry. What you up to?

Luke   I think rabbits or something have been at the flowerbeds. Look, half the bluebells've been ripped up, and the primroses are all gone, / and

Shadow   Oh, that was me.

Luke   What?

Shadow   I was studying them, and I thought maybe I was starting to see what you meant, about them being pretty to look at and nice to smell. So I picked a couple. So I could have them with me to look at whenever I want.

Luke   You can't do that.

Shadow   No?

Luke   'Cause then they die. And then no one else can look at them.

Shadow   Oh. Sorry.

Beat.

Shadow   Making a bit of a nuisance of myself today, aren't I?

Luke   Yeah.

Beat.

Shadow   Still. You must be pleased.

Luke   What?

Shadow   You were crapping yourself about all that getting your head ducked down the toilet at the comp. Must be a weight off, not having to worry about that any more.

Luke *looks at him.*

Shadow   You know, if you're all gonna be . . . (*He draws his finger across his throat.*)

Beat.

Luke   You didn't believe all that, did you?

Shadow   Well, yeah.

Luke   You mong.

Shadow   Didn't you believe it?

Luke   Why would I believe anything Katie Fletcher says?

Shadow   You reckon she made it up?

Luke   Well, obviously.

Shadow   What'd she do that for?

Luke (*beat*)   She thinks it's funny trying to frighten people.

Shadow   Well, that's not very good.

Luke   Well I know. Don't worry though – God'll sort her out.

Shadow   Mmm.

Luke   What?

Shadow   It's just –
– there is the air base. Full of Americans.
And the siren.

Luke   That's from the cheese factory / in Whitland.

Shadow   In Whitland, I know.
I heard what Nanna said.
I was listening.

Luke *looks at him.*

Shadow (*beat*)   It's a long way, for the sound to carry.
It'd make more sense if it came from the base.

Beat.

Luke   Obviously the bits are all there, aren't they?
If you're gonna tell a lie, you use bits of real things that're
round you.
You take bits of real things and you put them together the
wrong way and – you've got a lie.
You have to do it like that, otherwise – it'd just be obvious
you were lying, wouldn't it?

Shadow   You sound like – a bit of an expert, Luke.
You do a lot of lying, then?

Luke   I never tell a lie.

Shadow   Hear a lot of them, do you?

Beat.

Luke   No.

Beat.

Shadow   All right.
All right then.
It's just.
The other reason I don't think she made it up is –
(*He hesitates:* **Luke** *waits.*) – we've seen it before.
On dozens of worlds.
They can't quite make the leap to the next level – so they

blow themselves to bits . . .

You wouldn't even see the explosion. There'd be a flicker of light, then the heat would burn your optic nerve away and everything would go dark.

The eighty per cent of you that is water would flash to steam. Your fat would take a fraction longer to evaporate: you might even feel it sizzle for a moment before it fell away from your skeleton.

Your muscles would char, and your bones would blacken and turn to powder, and when the blast wave hit you'd crumble and be carried up into the atmosphere, maybe right to the edge of space.

Most of the powder that was you would fall straight back to earth. If you fell on land, the land would be poisoned. If you fell on people, cancers would grow where you touched them.

But some of you would hover up in the sky for a while.

You'd go sailing round the world, till finally gravity dragged you down. The last of you would flare and burn as you fell through the atmosphere, and maybe people on the ground would see you burn, and think you were a shooting star, and make a wish on you. And if they did, they would wish . . . to be dead.

(*Beat.*) All this, from splitting proton, from neutron, from electron.

The most basic structure.

Crack it, and out comes a force

That could consume you completely,

And leave just a shadow on the ground

To show where once a boy had been.

Shadow *steps close to him.*

Are you . . . going to cry, Luke?

He reaches out his hand to touch **Luke**'s *cheek and feel for tears.*
Beat.

Shadow   That's a relief then. You won't have to worry about the boys at the comp teasing you for being the last one to get hairs on your willy. 'Cause everybody's hair'll just be singed off, won't it.

Luke   Get lost.

Shadow   Only trying to look on the bright side.

He goes over to the flowerbed.

Actually, I think I will pull a few more of these flowers. I mean, I get what you're saying about leaving them for other people to see, but if they're just gonna get blown to bits I may as well take them back with me. Dry them. Put them in a museum.
'Cause we'll probably do that, we'll probably set up a museum about this place. Once you're all dead, like.

Katie *enters.*

Katie   My mum says I've gotta come and play with you for at least half an hour or there's no telly tonight.

Luke   Oh, lucky me.

Katie   Don't think I wanted to.

Luke   I don't.

Beat.

Katie   Is there any fish in this stream?

Luke   No.

Shadow   Yeah, and tell her why, Luke.

Katie *stares into the stream.*
Luke *stares at* **Katie**.
Eventually **Katie** *feels* **Luke**'s *gaze on the back of her head. She turns round.*

Katie   What?

Luke   You don't seem too bothered.

Katie   About what?

Luke   That we're all gonna be killed.

Katie (*beat*)   Everything dies, doesn't it.

Luke   Yeah, but . . .

Katie   But?

Beat.

Luke   Doesn't matter.

Shadow *watches* **Luke** *chicken out.*
He dumps his recorder, Polaroid, bits and bobs and walks over to **Luke** *and grabs him in a headlock.*

Shadow (*to* **Katie**)   But you'll have to watch your mum with her face all melted and her arms blown off, screaming and begging you to give her some water but you can't 'cause there's just these holes in her face, so you can't tell if you'd be pouring the water down her mouth or into her nose or into the spaces where her eyes used to be.

Luke *throws* **Shadow** *off.*

Katie   What'd you say that for?

Luke   I didn't say nothing!

Shadow   – and anyway all the water would be poison –

Katie *blocks her ears.*

Katie   I don't wanna hear –

Shadow   – and even if there was water that wasn't poison, you couldn't get it, cause your whole body's burnt so whenever you move it hurts so much you scream out you wanna die and your mum loves you and she can't bear to hear you screaming so she tries to clamp her hands over her ears but she can't cause her arms've been blown off so in the end all she can do is stand up and run against the wall and batter her head till she knocks herself out.

Katie   That is *horrible* . . .

Luke   Hadn't you ever thought about it?

Beat.

Katie   Not . . . like that.

Luke   But you knew. You knew all this stuff.

Katie   Yeah, but I didn't –

Shadow (*to* **Katie**)   It's not hard to put it together. Once
all the bits are in place.
(*Beat.*)
And you were calling me a rem.
You rem.

Katie   I just.
Didn't see it.

Shadow (*looks from* **Katie** *to* **Luke**)   Who'd want to see it?
You and the being you love most in the universe; the both of
you flayed; burned; dying.
I always wonder: does the screaming take over because the
physical agony stops you speaking, or just because . . . there
aren't the words.

Katie   I couldn't bear it, watching my mum die.

Shadow   You probably won't have to. Given an equal
dosing of the old glow-in-the-dark rays, the kids tend to go
first. The less your body mass, the less you can take. So
probably it'll be your mum who gets to watch you die. And
that way she'll see what's coming to her. Lots of parents say
the watery vomiting is the most distressing stage, 'cause it's
just like when their little baby had a tummy bug and they
think . . . they can't help but delude themselves you're going
to get better.
Until of course, your teeth start to fall out and your gums
turn to mush and you start to bleed from everywhere /

Katie   Or if I went first. Knowing I was dying and my
mum watching me and knowing what she was going
through 'cause she couldn't help me.

Shadow *peers at* **Katie**

Shadow   She's crying!

Luke   Katie.
Katie.
It's all right.

Katie   Why is it like this?

Luke   Look at me: am I afraid? Am I crying?

Katie *looks at him; shakes her head.*

Luke   I'm not.
'Cause there's nothing to cry about.
Everything that happens, even if it seems really bad, it's for the best.
'Cause that's the way God plans it.

Katie   Even this?

Luke   Even this.

Katie   How can this be for the best?

Luke   Well, it's like – like with the Good Samaritan, he wouldn't have had the chance to be good if the Syrian hadn't got beaten up by the robbers.
When bad things happen, it's to give us a chance to make things better.

Katie   When we're all burned and screaming and there's no one coming to save us?

Beat.
Luke *hasn't got an answer.* **Katie** *turns away.*

Luke   Katie, please don't cry /

Shadow   Nanna would know.

Luke *looks at him.*

Shadow   She'll understand it.
If anybody does.

Beat.

Luke (*to* **Katie**)   I'll ask my nanna. She's bound to understand.

Katie   D'you think so?

Luke   For definite.

Katie   What can she say?

Luke   I don't know. But – she'll explain it.

Katie   And you'll explain it to me?

Luke   And then you won't have to worry.

Shadow   About the blistering, and the bubbling /

Luke *silences him with a stare.*

Katie   I'd better go.
(*Beat.*) I'm scared to go home.
I'm scared in case it happens tonight. What if it happens tonight and we all get burned and my mum's crying 'cause she knows she's gonna have to watch me die – and I won't know what to say to stop her crying. I won't know what to tell her so she'll understand it's all okay.

Luke   It won't happen tonight, Katie, I promise you.
I'll ask my Nanna and she'll explain it to me and I'll tell you tomorrow and then it'll all be fine. And there'll be no reason to cry.

Beat.

Katie   All right then.

Katie *leaves.*

Shadow   Nicely done, Luke. I think you fooled her.

Luke   I didn't fool her about nothing.

Shadow   Oh no?

Luke   I'm gonna ask Nanna, and she's gonna explain it.

Shadow   You . . . actually think she will?

Luke   Of course.

Shadow   You think she'll have an explanation.

Luke   I know she will.

Shadow   Star Cadet Luke, you are bloody priceless. Glactic Centre are gonna piss themselves.

Scene Nine

Shadow *skulks, tape-recording the conversation.*

Nanna   I saw you playing with Katie this afternoon.

Luke   Was for a bit.

Nanna   She didn't – do anything?

Luke   No.

Nanna   So you're all right, then?

Luke   Yes.

Nanna   It's just you don't seem / like

Luke   I'm fine.

Beat.

Nanna   Well, now I know there's something wrong, don't I. You're such a good boy ordinarily, I don't know that I could say I know how it looks when you tell a lie, because I can hardly recall an occasion when you've lied to your Nanna.
But I know how it looks when you're not happy.

Beat.

Nanna   I'll just sit here, then, till you decide to tell me.

Luke   Nanna, it's –
– it's something awful, Nanna.

Nanna   We won't know that until we hear it.

Luke   I don't wanna say.

Nanna   Well –
– hold on. It's not Wednesday, is it?

Luke (*shakes his head*)   Why?

Nanna   Just the Lord Jesus left me a note saying that Wednesdays this month were going to be really busy for him, so on Wednesdays he wouldn't be able to help me sort out your problems.
But given that it isn't a Wednesday: do you really think there is anything that me and the Lord Jesus can't sort out between us?

Luke   No.

Nanna   No. Let's have it then, so I can be off to my bed.

Beat.

Shadow   Go on, then.

Beat.

Luke (*to* **Shadow**)   What if she hasn't got an answer?

Shadow   Of course she'll have an answer.

Luke   You think?

Shadow   For definite.
(*Beat.*) She'll make one up.
She'll tell you a story
To make you feel better.
(*Beat.*) She'll lie.

Beat.

Shadow   Don't you think it'd be useful to know how it looks when your nanna lies to you?
Don't you think you should learn to read the signs?

Luke *can't answer.*

Shadow   You have to ask her.
You told Katie you would.
Nanna'll tell you a story, then you can tell it to Katie and everything'll be fine again.

Nanna   Luke?

Beat.

Luke   All my bottles – I think I've driven the fish out of the river.

Nanna *looks at him carefully.*

Luke   'Cause I've taken the bottles, now the fish have got nowhere to live and so they've all gone /

Nanna   Is that what you're worried about?

Luke *nods.*

Shadow   Oh, I see: you don't need to learn
How it looks when your nanna lies to you.

Nanna   Oh, you daft little thing. Of course you haven't driven the fish out of the river.

Shadow   You don't need to learn how it looks when your nanna lies to you –

Nanna   That's all you were worried about?

Shadow   – because you learned that ages ago.

Luke   No.

Nanna   Well, what then?

Shadow   He wants to know why God's gonna let them blow / up the world.

Luke   Shut up!

Luke *dives on* **Shadow**.
They wrestle.

Nanna   Luke! Luke!

Shadow *breaks free from* **Luke** *and runs away.*

Nanna   What on earth is wrong with you, lovely?

Luke *goes to speak.*
Changes his mind.
He picks himself up and dusts himself off.

Luke   It's nothing, Nanna.
I'm fine. Don't upset yourself.
It's nothing for you to worry about.

Scene Ten

Luke *sits up in bed in the dark.*
Shadow *sits at the other end of the bed with all his apparatus.*

Shadow   So – nervous?

Luke *shakes his head.*

Beat.

In the distance, a siren.

Shadow   Here we go . . .

Shadow *starts taking pictures of* **Luke**'s *face.*

Nervous yet, Luke?

Luke   No.

Shadow   The bombs are on their way, Luke.

Luke   The Lord wouldn't do that to us.

Shadow   Two minutes to go, matey boy.

Luke   I'm not listening . . .

Shadow *grabs his mike and thrusts it into his face.*

Shadow   Any last thoughts you'd like to share with Glactic civilization?

Luke   Rhubarb-rhubarb-rhubarb-rhubarb-rhubarb –

Shadow   What's that sound?

Luke   – rhubarb-rhubarb-rhubarb-rhubarb –

Shadow   I think I can actually hear the bombs whistling through the air.

Luke   Our Father which art in heaven hallowed be Thy Name –

Shadow (*taking a snap*)   I'm gonna call that one 'A primitive biped wards off fusion bombs by means of ritual chant'. Unless you can think of something snappier?

Luke   – Thy Kingdom come, Thy Will be done –

Shadow   That's right, Lukey: His will be done. He wants this, He wants this to happen. He wants this to happen to you. He loves you *that much.*

Luke *pulls up.* **Shadow** *freezes, stares at him.*

Shadow   Well, bloody hell.

Shadow *peers forward. He reaches into his pockets, pulls out a cotton bud and a test tube.*
He leans forward and wipes the cotton bud under **Luke***'s eyes. He looks at the bud, then puts the bud into the test tube.*

Shadow   A tear, Luke.

He holds another bud ready. No further teardrops emerge.

One single, solitary tear.
Is that the best you can do?
Cause it can get worse yet, Luke.
It can still get worse, if it has to.

Scene Eleven

Luke *and* **Katie** *are bouncing a beach ball between them.*
Shadow *comes into the garden with them.*

Luke   D'you know, the sky over the Preseli Mountains goes exactly the same colours every night.

Katie   I've decided where I want to be when it happens.

Luke   It goes red, but not like red sauce, more like rust; then it goes purple, like cherry Space Dust.

Katie   I want to be at school. At the comp. First, 'cause if I'm there, then mum won't have to see me burned and crying.

Luke   Then purple turns to blue, the colour that Nanna calls navy blue, even though it isn't blue like pictures of the sea.

Katie   And, second, 'cause there's this basement below the metalwork block, and I don't think the caretakers know the lock is broken.

Luke   But maybe the sea is that colour blue, when you're in a submarine, miles under the water

Katie   I'll show it you when you come to school. If you ever do.

Luke   Then it goes black, which is just like black.

Katie   And if I got down into the basement, I reckon I wouldn't take such a massive dose.

Luke   Then at about four in the morning, the black starts to turn back into blue.

Katie   So I'd live a bit longer, which would be awful, of course.

Luke   Then the blue fades to grey, then the sun comes and fries the grey red again. It's exactly the same, every night.
(*Beat.*) And I really wish it would change. Just some variety would be nice.

Katie   But at least I could come up and watch Paul Matthews and Dave Barclay and Arthur Morris and all those bastards die.

Luke *looks at her.*

Katie   What?

Luke   Nothing.

Katie   What?

Luke *grabs for the ball but knocks it away. He goes chasing after it.*

Shadow (*to* **Katie**)   It's just I heard them lot all talking about you the other day.

Luke *returns with the ball.*

Katie   When?

Luke *doesn't want to say.*

Katie   When'd you hear them?

Luke   The other day. I was under the bridge, and they were all talking about you.

Katie   What'd they say?

Luke *says nothing; bounces the ball back to her.*

Katie   They talk bollocks, you know. You can't believe a word they say.

She throws the ball to **Luke***;* **Shadow** *swoops in and intercepts.*

Shadow   Arthur Morris said he had three fingers up you Friday night.

He passes the ball back to **Katie***. She turns away.*

Luke   Paul Barclay said he was gonna have a go this Friday night.

Beat.

And he reckoned he was gonna get four.

Beat.

Four fingers. Up you.

Beat.

What does that mean, Katie?

Katie   It means /

Luke   'Cause I thought you didn't like them.
I thought you wanted to spend your last hours on earth
watching them die.

Katie   I wait for the siren. And when the siren comes, I
freeze up, and I sit there –

Luke   – waiting to be killed.

Katie   And I can't bear it. Not all the time.

Luke   I bear it.

Katie   And there's things you can do . . . that stop you
thinking about it. Just for a little while, just for a couple of
seconds.

Luke   And you do them with Arthur Morris.

Katie   And Paul Barclay and Davy Matthews and anyone.
Just to stop thinking about it.

Luke   With anyone?

Katie   Anyone.

Luke   With *anyone*?

Beat.

Katie   You'd say it would upset God.

Shadow   I don't think I care about that any more.

Luke   I don't think . . .
I want to play with you any more.

Shadow *slumps.*

Scene Twelve

Luke *and* **Nanna** *are at the table.* **Shadow** *watches.*

Luke   I hate liver and onions.

Nanna   That's a pity.
They're terribly fond of you.

Luke   Could I just eat the onions?

Nanna   'Course you can.

Luke   And then have bread and butter to fill up on?

Nanna   So long as you finish the liver before you start on the onions.

Luke   That's not fair.

Nanna   Nor will you be, after I lock you in the coalshed.

Luke   You can try.

Nanna *looks up sharply.* **Luke** *can't hold her gaze.*

Nanna   I think you've been spending a bit too much time in the company of Katie Fletcher.

Luke *prods miserably at his liver.*

Nanna   Just try to eat most of it. It'll help you grow up big and strong.
Those boys at the comp won't be able to scare you then.

She gets on with her food.
Luke *stares at her for a beat. Then looks over at* **Shadow**.
Shadow *walks over to the table, picks up* **Luke**'s *plate, and very deliberately drops it on the floor.*

Nanna   What in heaven's name did you do that for?

Luke   I'm not scared of the comp boys. I'm gonna watch them all die.

Nanna   You get to your room, now. Don't let me ever hear you saying such things again.

Luke *starts towards his bedroom.*

Nanna   I'm at a loss with you, Luke Evans. I try my best and it seems to go to nothing.
(*Beat.*) Just you go to bed, and pray, and think long and hard about the way you're behaving lately.

She seems to have finished. **Luke** *starts again towards his room.*

You're family, and I'll always love you. But I don't think I like you very much these days.

Luke (*beat*)   If you don't like me . . . why don't you get rid of me?

Scene Thirteen

Katie *comes into the garden with some blankets.*
She sits down, arranges the blankets around her.
Luke's *sat up in bed,* **Shadow** *sitting at the far end.*

Shadow   Homes?
I don't get it. It's a new concept.

Luke   Where kids go. When their families can't cope with them.

Shadow   What're they like?

Luke   Horrible.
But if you're in one of them, it means your family don't have to watch you die.

Shadow   Right –
– smart.
So the families struggle with the kids for as long as they can bear, then package them off to these . . . 'homes'.

Luke   Yeah.

Shadow   And can they have more kids then, if they want?

Luke   Well . . . I don't know.
I s'pose.

Shadow   Amazing.
You know, when I first got here, I looked around and I
thought – what the hell are all the grown-ups doing? All this
frantic activity, and when you figure it out, it's all for crap.
Back where I come from, we're exploring the galaxy and
figuring out the secrets of the universe and unearthing the
ruins of ancient civilizations and down here you're all –
rushing around and trying to scrape together the cash for a
Betamax. And it's all bollocks.
(*Beat.*) But this is a subtle planet.
It's not all how it seems on the surface. That stuff with the
food all the grown-ups do –

Luke   – cooking it, you mean?

Shadow   – yeah, and, arguing about what you watch on
the telly – what's that about? And *money*! All these little
tokens floating around, and all the energy that takes up,
worrying about paying the mortgage and worrying about
paying the rent, and worrying about the job, and worrying
about being on the dole.
But I just didn't see –
– the beauty of it all.
(*He looks to* **Luke**.) You know what it's really all about, don't
you?

Luke *shakes his head.*

Shadow   It's so they don't have to be like you.
They fill their heads up with all this crap
So they don't have to lie awake night after night
Waiting for the siren –

Luke   – waiting to be killed.

Shadow   Exactly!
And – oh, oh, this is incredible! – and *that's* why they have
kids at all – to give themselves more to get worked up about.
So they get to stamp around downstairs fuming about being

at the end of their tether and where did they go wrong and
what they hell are they going to do –
– while you lie awake in bed, shitting yourselves: so they
don't have to.

Beat.

Why didn't you tell me that's all you kids were for?
I wouldn't have wasted my time, I'd've gone straight to a
grown-up.
(*Beat: he studies* **Luke**.) 'Cause . . . you did understand that,
didn't you, Luke?
I mean, you must've put all the pieces together.
A bright boy like you.

Luke *gets out of bed.*

Shadow   What you doing?

Luke   Katie said you could climb down the porch roof
from my window.

Luke *goes over to* **Katie** *in the garden.* **Shadow** *comes over and
watches.*

Katie   I thought you were never coming.

Luke *doesn't answer.*

Katie   D'you wanna get under here?

She holds open the blanket for him. He doesn't move.

Luke   The siren's late tonight, isn't it?

Katie   D'you think that means anything?

Luke (*beat*)   They might not test it if they knew they were
gonna have to use it for real later.

Katie   Don't say that /

Luke   Arthur Morris, though. He's horrible.

Katie   I know.

Luke   When Arthur Morris was in our school, he never
used to wash his hands after he'd been to toilet. He used to
chase people around, saying he had all . . . poo on his
hands. If he caught you he'd wipe his hands in your face
and say you had his poo on your face. He'd stick his fingers
in your mouth and say you were eating his poo /

Katie   I can't remember the last time I slept, Luke.

Luke   Me neither.

Katie   If you came under here with me, maybe we'd be
able to.

Luke   I don't think Nanna'd like it.

Katie   No.

Luke   I don't think God'd be very happy with me, neither.

Katie   I don't s'pose he would, no.

Katie *holds open the blanket.*
Shadow *watches.*
In the bedroom: **Nanna** *enters and sees the empty bed.*
In the distance, the siren goes.
Luke *and* **Katie** *stare at one another.*

Katie   Luke. Will you – (*Reaches out to him.*)

Nanna   Oh God please, let him come back to me –

Shadow *spots* **Nanna**.
He walks back to the bedroom.

Nanna   – I know it's a sin to test You Lord but please just
bring him back safe to me –

Shadow *stands and watches her.*
The siren falls silent.
Nanna *listens intently.*

Katie   Luke – if we don't go straight away – you won't
leave me, will you?

Luke   Of course not.

Katie   D'you promise?

Luke *says nothing.*

Katie   If this is it, and we're burned, you won't leave me.

Luke   I promise.

Katie   You won't leave me, hurt and on my own.

Luke   I won't.

Katie   You won't let me die alone.

Luke *looks at her.*

Nanna   Bring him back and I swear I'll never, never speak like that to him again . . .

Shadow   But obviously you will. And if I can see that, then presumably so can the Lord. He knows you're lying to him.

Nanna   I mean it, Lord. Never a harsh word from me again.

Nanna *waits for an answer.*

Shadow   Fine.
Fine, if that's the way you want it.

Shadow *steps towards her.*
He reaches out, and touches his finger just above her left breast.
Nanna *gasps in pain and falls to the bed.*
Shadow *stands over her.*

Shadow   Don't you fucking cry now, you asked for that.

Katie   You won't leave me.

Beat.

You won't leave me burned and crying and on my own.

Luke   I think I heard my Nanna.

Katie   Luke!

Shadow   No!

Katie   You promised.

Luke *runs.*
He goes to **Nanna**, *lying on his bed.*
Shadow *watches.*

Luke   Nanna?
(*Beat.*) Nanna, are you all right?

Nanna   I came in and your bed was empty, and I was worried sick /

Luke   I'm sorry, I couldn't sleep, I went for a walk.

Nanna   Thank God you're all right.
(*She hugs him again.*) I don't know what I'd do /

Luke   The woods and the river looked so pretty, I wanted to have a wander round. See it all properly.

Nanna   I thought –
– I don't know what I thought.

Shadow *turns away; goes over to* **Katie**.

Shadow   Listen: you just sit tight there, and I'll fetch him back now.

Nanna   Lay down now, and I'll tuck you in.

Luke *gets into bed and lies down.*

Nanna   Promise me you'll stay away from that Katie.

Luke   Nanna –

Nanna   It's not that she's – she's not a bad girl, it's just . . . There's things you're too young for.

Luke   I promise, Nanna.

Beat.

Nanna   All right, then.
Goodnight.

Luke Night-night, Nanna.

Nanna *goes to leave. She pauses.*

Nanna You don't want . . . you don't want Nanna to sleep in with you tonight, do you, if you're having trouble dropping off?

Luke I'll be fine, Nanna.

Nanna 'Course you will.

She leaves. **Shadow** *comes over.*

Shadow She's crying.

Luke I can't.

Shadow Really badly.

Luke I promised Nanna.

Shadow You promised Katie first.

Luke *doesn't answer.*

Shadow She needs you.

Luke I can't.

Shadow And you need her more.

Beat.

Luke I promised my Nanna.

They look at each other.

Shadow This is not how it's supposed to be.

Luke I know.

Beat.

Shadow Fine. If that's the way you want / it.

Luke / It's not.
It's not the way I want it at all.

Shadow *turns and walks back to* **Katie**.

Shadow *stands over* **Katie**.
Eventually **Katie** *looks up at him.*

Shadow   Look. I'm sorry.
This has
Really not gone according to plan.
But – they're not going to beam me back
Till they get the signal for mission complete, so
I'm fucked too, you know.

Katie   So will you stay?

Shadow   Me? I can't *stay*.
No, that's not my mission, you don't –

Katie   If I'm burned, will you hold me?

Shadow (*beat*)   You don't get it at all.

Katie   Will you find the bits of me that aren't burned, and
hold me?

Shadow   No, that's not my mission.
I'm not equipped for any of that. (*He looks to* **Luke**.)

Luke   They're called forensic scientists.
The people who find out what happened
In crashes and murders and things.
They talked to my Nanna.
Smiling when they looked down at me.
But very very serious when they talked to Nanna.
(*Beat.*) I was tiny then, clinging on to Nanna's legs.
They must have thought I . . . couldn't hear.
They must've thought I couldn't put the words together.
(*Beat.*) They told Nanna that the way the car crashed had
trapped my mum inside.
The steering wheel was crushed into her chest, and her legs
were gone through the dash.
But my dad, he could get out.
He crawled out of the window and got free.
(*Beat.*) And then he crawled back in.
He got back in so he was killed when it all exploded.

And he never came to check on me.
(*Beat.*) He wanted to come and check on me, I know.
But with all them bits of car in her and broken glass
everywhere, and petrol, and her in pain and knowing she
was gonna die – he couldn't let my mummy go through that
alone.
And so he had to leave me alone.
(*Beat.*) That wasn't how things were supposed to be, I know.
But that was the best. That was the best he could manage.

Shadow   That's not my mission.
I'm not equipped.

Katie *moves closer to* **Shadow**.
Shadow *doesn't move away.*
Katie *reaches out to hold him.*

Shadow   I'm not – for this.

Katie *stops.*

I'm just a trick of the light.

Katie *looks at him.*
She takes his hand.

Methuen Modern Plays

include work by

Jean Anouilh
John Arden
Margaretta D'Arcy
Peter Barnes
Sebastian Barry
Brendan Behan
Dermot Bolger
Edward Bond
Bertolt Brecht
Howard Brenton
Anthony Burgess
Simon Burke
Jim Cartwright
Caryl Churchill
Noël Coward
Lucinda Coxon
Sarah Daniels
Nick Darke
Nick Dear
Shelagh Delaney
David Edgar
David Eldridge
Dario Fo
Michael Frayn
John Godber
Paul Godfrey
David Greig
John Guare
Peter Handke
David Harrower
Jonathan Harvey
Iain Heggie
Declan Hughes
Terry Johnson
Sarah Kane
Charlotte Keatley
Barrie Keeffe
Howard Korder

Robert Lepage
Stephen Lowe
Doug Lucie
Martin McDonagh
John McGrath
Terrence McNally
David Mamet
Patrick Marber
Arthur Miller
Mtwa, Ngema & Simon
Tom Murphy
Phyllis Nagy
Peter Nichols
Joseph O'Connor
Joe Orton
Louise Page
Joe Penhall
Luigi Pirandello
Stephen Poliakoff
Franca Rame
Mark Ravenhill
Philip Ridley
Reginald Rose
David Rudkin
Willy Russell
Jean-Paul Sartre
Sam Shepard
Wole Soyinka
Shelagh Stephenson
C. P. Taylor
Theatre de Complicite
Theatre Workshop
Sue Townsend
Judy Upton
Timberlake Wertenbaker
Roy Williams
Victoria Wood

Methuen Contemporary Dramatists
include

Peter Barnes (three volumes)
Sebastian Barry
Edward Bond (six volumes)
Howard Brenton
  (two volumes)
Richard Cameron
Jim Cartwright
Caryl Churchill (two volumes)
Sarah Daniels (two volumes)
Nick Darke
David Edgar (three volumes)
Ben Elton
Dario Fo (two volumes)
Michael Frayn (two volumes)
Paul Godfrey
John Guare
Peter Handke
Jonathan Harvey
Declan Hughes
Terry Johnson (two volumes)
Bernard-Marie Koltès
David Lan
Bryony Lavery
Doug Lucie
David Mamet (three volumes)

Martin McDonagh
Duncan McLean
Anthony Minghella
  (two volumes)
Tom Murphy (four volumes)
Phyllis Nagy
Anthony Nielsen
Philip Osment
Louise Page
Joe Penhall
Stephen Poliakoff
  (three volumes)
Christina Reid
Philip Ridley
Willy Russell
Ntozake Shange
Sam Shepard (two volumes)
Wole Soyinka (two volumes)
David Storey (three volumes)
Sue Townsend
Michel Vinaver (two volumes)
Michael Wilcox
David Wood (two volumes)
Victoria Wood

For a complete catalogue of Methuen Drama titles
write to:

Methuen Drama
215 Vauxhall Bridge Road
London SW1V 1EJ

or you can visit our website at:

www.methuen.co.uk